Cool TREATS & SWEETS

Easy & Fun Comfort Food

ALEX KUSKOWSKI

Checkerboard Library

An Imprint of Abdo Publishing
www.abdopublishing.com

www.abdopublishing.com

Published by Abdo Publishing, a division of ABDO, PO Box 398166, Minneapolis, Minnesota 55439. Copyright © 2015 by Abdo Consulting Group, Inc. International copyrights reserved in all countries. No part of this book may be reproduced in any form without written permission from the publisher. Checkerboard Library™ is a trademark and logo of Abdo Publishing.

Printed in the United States of America, North Mankato, Minnesota
102014
012015

THIS BOOK CONTAINS
RECYCLED MATERIALS

Editor: Liz Salzmann
Content Developer: Nancy Tuminelly
Cover and Interior Design and Production:
Colleen Dolphin, Mighty Media, Inc.
Food Production: Frankie Tuminelly
Photo Credits: Colleen Dolphin, Shutterstock

The following manufacturers/names appearing in this book are trademarks: Argo®, Arm & Hammer®, Gold Medal®, Kemps®, Kraft® Calumet®, Land O Lakes®, Oster®, Pyrex®, Roundy's®

Library of Congress Cataloging-in-Publication Data
Kuskowski, Alex.
  Cool treats & sweets : easy & fun comfort food / Alex Kuskowski.
    pages cm. -- (Cool home cooking)
  Audience: Ages 7-14.
  Includes index.
  ISBN 978-1-62403-505-0
  1. Desserts--Juvenile literature. I. Title. II. Title: Cool treats and sweets.
  TX773.K757 2015
  641.86--dc23
                    2014024640

SAFETY FIRST!

Some recipes call for activities or ingredients that require caution. If you see these symbols, ask an adult for help.

HOT STUFF!
This recipe requires the use of a stove or oven. Always use pot holders when handling hot objects.

SUPER SHARP!
This recipe includes the use of a sharp **utensil** such as a knife or grater.

NUT ALERT!
Some people can get very sick if they eat nuts. If you cook something with nuts, let people know!

CONTENTS

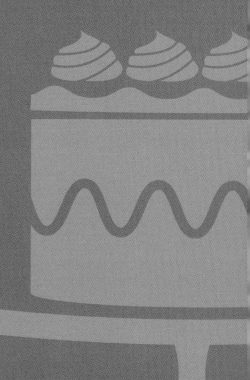

DELIGHT WITH DESSERTS!

Surprise your friends and family by making homemade **desserts**! Homemade desserts are special treats. They taste and smell great. Try making cake, pudding, and trifle.

Cooking food at home is healthy and tasty. It can be a lot of fun too. Many canned or frozen foods include unhealthy ingredients. When you make the food, you know exactly what's in it. It's easy to make a dish that's **unique** to you. Cook a recipe just the way you like it. Add fresh ingredients to make flavors pop. You can even share what you make with others.

Put the flavor back in your food. Start making home-cooked meals! Learn how to serve up some **delicious** desserts for your next meal. Check out the recipes in this book.

THE BASICS

Get your cooking started off right with these basic tips!

ASK PERMISSION

Before you cook, ask **permission** to use the kitchen, cooking tools, and ingredients. If you'd like to do something yourself, say so! Just remember to be safe. If you would like help, ask for it! Always get help when you are using a stove or oven.

BE PREPARED

Be organized. Knowing where everything is makes cooking easier and more fun!

Read the directions all the way through before you start. Remember to follow the directions in order.

The most important ingredient in great cooking is preparation! Make sure you have everything you'll need.

Put each ingredient in a separate bowl before starting.

BE SMART, BE SAFE

Always have an adult nearby for hot jobs, such as using the oven or stove.

Have an adult around when using a sharp tool, such as a knife or grater. Always be careful when using them!

Remember to turn pot handles toward the back of the stove. That way you avoid accidentally knocking them over.

BE NEAT, BE CLEAN

Start with clean hands, clean tools, and a clean work surface.

Tie back long hair so it stays out of the food.

Wear comfortable clothing and roll up long sleeves.

COOL COOKING TERMS

HERE ARE SOME HELPFUL TERMS YOU NEED TO KNOW!

CHOP

Chop means to cut into small pieces.

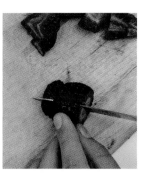

BOIL

Boil means to heat liquid until it begins to bubble.

COAT

Coat means to cover something with another ingredient or mixture.

CHILL

Chill means to put something in a refrigerator for a while.

CREAM

Cream means to beat butter and sugar together until it's light and **fluffy**.

DRIZZLE

Drizzle means to slowly pour a liquid over something.

SPREAD

Spread means to make a smooth layer with a **utensil**.

GREASE

Grease means to coat something with butter, oil, or cooking spray.

STIR

Stir means to mix ingredients together, usually with a large spoon.

PEEL

Peel means to remove the skin, often with a peeler.

WHISK

Whisk means to beat quickly by hand with a whisk or a fork.

COOL TOOLS

HERE ARE SOME OF THE TOOLS YOU WILL NEED!

8 × 8-inch baking dish

aluminum foil

cutting board

electric mixer

glass serving dishes

measuring cups

measuring spoons

microwave-safe bowl

mixing bowls

mixing spoon

parchment paper

pie plate

saucepan

pot holders

rubber spatula

sharp knife

whisk

COOL INGREDIENTS

HERE ARE SOME OF THE INGREDIENTS YOU WILL NEED!

baking powder

baking soda	blackberries	blueberries	brown sugar
butter	buttermilk	chocolate chips	cinnamon
cocoa	cornstarch	eggs	flour

graham crackers

heavy cream

lemon juice

maple syrup

milk

mini marshmallows

nutmeg

peaches

piecrust

raspberries

rhubarb

rolled oats

strawberries

white sugar

vanilla extract

vanilla ice cream

SWEET VANILLA PUDDING

Try this simply smooth treat!

 MAKES 4 SERVINGS

INGREDIENTS

3 tablespoons cornstarch

2/3 cup sugar

1/4 teaspoon salt

2 1/3 cups milk

1 1/4 teaspoons vanilla extract

1 3/4 tablespoons butter

TOOLS

measuring cups

measuring spoons

small mixing bowl

whisk

saucepan

mixing spoon

pot holders

glass serving dishes

1. Put the cornstarch, sugar, salt, and 1/3 cup milk in a small bowl. Whisk until there are no lumps.

2. Put the remaining milk in a saucepan. Stir and heat the milk over medium-low heat until it begins to steam.

3. Add the cornstarch mixture to the saucepan. Cook 5 minutes, stirring constantly.

4. Turn the heat down to very low. Add the vanilla and butter. Stir and cook 5 minutes.

5. Pour the pudding into a medium mixing bowl. Cover the bowl with plastic wrap. Chill for 2 hours.

TIP

Make your pudding chocolate! Add 2 tablespoons of cocoa powder in step 1.

TART BLUEBERRY CAKE

Get ready to be a berry baker!

MAKES 9 SERVINGS

INGREDIENTS

non-stick cooking spray
½ cup butter
1 cup white sugar
¼ teaspoon salt
2 teaspoons vanilla extract
2 eggs
1½ cup plus 1 tablespoon flour
1 teaspoon baking powder
⅓ cup milk
1½ cup blueberries
2 tablespoons brown sugar

TOOLS

measuring cups
measuring spoons
8 × 8-inch baking dish
mixing bowls
electric mixer
whisk
mixing spoon
pot holders

1 Preheat the oven to 350 degrees. Grease the baking dish with cooking spray.

2 Cream the butter and ½ cup white sugar in a large mixing bowl. Add the salt and vanilla extract. Stir.

3 Separate the eggs. Put the whites in a small bowl. Set them aside. Add the yolks to the butter mixture. Whisk until creamy.

4 Stir the baking powder and 1½ cups flour into the butter mixture.

5 Put the berries and 1 tablespoon flour in a small mixing bowl. Stir to coat the berries with flour. Add the berries to the **batter**. Stir to mix in the berries.

6 Whisk the egg whites until they are thick. Whisk in the remaining white sugar one tablespoon at a time. Add the egg mixture to the batter. Stir well.

7 Pour the batter into the baking dish. Sprinkle the brown sugar over the top. Bake 50 minutes.

5

6

7

RASPBERRY ICE CREAM PIE

Chow down on this berry tasty pie!

MAKES 8 SERVINGS

INGREDIENTS

1¼ cups graham cracker crumbs

⅓ cup butter, softened

¼ cup sugar

1 cup heavy whipping cream

2 tablespoons powdered sugar

1 quart vanilla ice cream, softened

2 cups raspberries

TOOLS

measuring cups

measuring spoons

mixing bowls

mixing spoon

pie plate

whisk

rubber spatula

1 Put the graham cracker crumbs, butter, and sugar in a mixing bowl. Stir well. Press the mixture into the bottom and sides of the pie plate. Freeze for 10 minutes.

2 Put the whipping cream and powdered sugar in a large mixing bowl. Whisk until the mixture becomes thick.

3 Spread a layer of ice cream on the graham cracker crust. Put a layer of raspberries on top of the ice cream. Fill the rest of the crust with ice cream.

4 Spread the whipping cream over the ice cream. Top with extra raspberries. Freeze for 2 hours. Let it sit out 10 minutes before serving.

VANILLA BERRY TRIFLE

Serve up a creative treat!

 MAKES 6 JARS

INGREDIENTS

vanilla pudding (see recipe on page 14)

CAKE

non-stick cooking spray

1 cup sugar

½ cup butter

2 eggs

2 teaspoons vanilla extract

1½ cups flour

2 teaspoons baking powder

¾ cup whole milk

½ cup blueberries

½ cup chopped strawberries

½ cup blackberries

TOPPING

1 cup heavy whipping cream

2 tablespoons white sugar

1 teaspoon vanilla extract

TOOLS

measuring cups

measuring spoons

sharp knife

cutting board

8 × 8-inch baking dish

mixing bowls

whisk

mixing spoon

6 mason jars

pot holders

1. Preheat the oven to 350 degrees. Grease the baking dish with cooking spray.

2. Cream the sugar and butter together in a medium mixing bowl. Add the eggs and vanilla extract. Whisk for 10 minutes.

3. Stir in the flour and baking powder. Add the milk. Stir well. Pour the **batter** into the baking pan. Bake 35 minutes. Let the cake cool.

4. Make the topping. Whisk together the topping ingredients in a medium bowl.

5. Stir the fruit together in a bowl.

6. Cut the cake into 1-inch (2.5 cm) cubes.

7. Put a layer of cake cubes in each jar. Put 2 tablespoons of fruit over the cake. Put 2 tablespoons of pudding over the fruit. Spread the pudding evenly. Repeat the layers of cake, fruit, and pudding. Top each jar with 2 tablespoons whipped topping.

PERFECT PEACH COBBLER

Make a yummy classic everyone will love!

MAKES 9 SERVINGS

1. Preheat the oven to 425 degrees.

2. Put all of the filling ingredients in a large mixing bowl. Stir to coat the peaches evenly.

3. Spread the filling evenly in the baking dish. Bake 10 minutes. Let it cool.

4. Make the topping. Put the cinnamon and 7 tablespoons white sugar in a small mixing bowl. Stir.

5. Put the flour, brown sugar, baking soda, salt, butter, and remaining white sugar in a medium mixing bowl. Stir well. Whisk in ¼ cup boiling water.

6. Cover the peaches with the flour mixture. Sprinkle the cinnamon mixture on top. Bake 30 minutes.

INGREDIENTS

FILLING

6 peaches, peeled and chopped

¼ cup white sugar

¼ cup brown sugar

½ teaspoon cinnamon

¼ teaspoon nutmeg

1 teaspoon lemon juice

4 teaspoons cornstarch

TOPPING

3 teaspoons cinnamon

11 tablespoons white sugar

1 cup flour

¼ cup brown sugar

1 teaspoon baking soda

½ teaspoon salt

8 tablespoons butter, chopped

TOOLS

peeler

sharp knife

cutting board

measuring cups

measuring spoons

8 × 8-inch baking dish

mixing bowls

mixing spoon

whisk

pot holders

22

VELVETY CHOCOLATE CAKE

Grab a bite of this cake!

MAKES 12 SERVINGS

INGREDIENTS

CAKE

2 cups flour

2 cups white sugar

½ teaspoon cinnamon

¼ teaspoon salt

1 cup butter

½ cup cocoa powder

½ cup buttermilk

2 eggs

1 teaspoon baking soda

1¼ teaspoon vanilla extract

FROSTING

½ cup butter, melted

6 tablespoons buttermilk

4 cups powdered sugar

1½ teaspoon vanilla extract

TOOLS

measuring cups

measuring spoons

mixing bowls

mixing spoons

saucepan

whisk

8 × 8-inch baking dish

rubber spatula

pot holders

---

1 Preheat the oven to 350 degrees. Put the flour, sugar, cinnamon, and salt in a large mixing bowl. Stir well.

2 Melt the butter in a saucepan. Stir in the cocoa powder and 1 cup hot water. Heat the mixture for 30 seconds. Pour the butter mixture over the flour mixture. Stir well.

3 Add the buttermilk, eggs, baking soda, and vanilla extract. Whisk together.

4 Pour the **batter** into the baking dish. Spread it evenly with a rubber spatula. Bake 20 minutes. Let the cake cool.

5 In a small mixing bowl, whisk together the frosting ingredients. Pour the frosting over the cake. Spread it evenly with a rubber spatula.

RHUBARB BERRY PIE

The perfect combination of sweet and tart!

 MAKES 8 SERVINGS

INGREDIENTS

non-stick cooking spray
9-inch piecrust
1 cup white sugar
1¼ cup flour
3 cups chopped rhubarb
3 cups chopped strawberries
1 cup brown sugar
¼ cup butter
½ teaspoon cinnamon

TOOLS

measuring cups
measuring spoons
sharp knife
cutting board
pie plate
mixing bowls
mixing spoons
aluminum foil
pot holders

1 Preheat the oven to 425 degrees. Grease the pie plate with cooking spray. Place the piecrust in the pie plate.

2 Put the white sugar and ¼ cup flour in a large mixing bowl. Stir. Add the rhubarb and berries. Stir to coat the rhubarb and berries. Let it sit 30 minutes. Pour the rhubarb mixture into the pie plate.

3 Put the brown sugar, butter, cinnamon, and 1 cup flour in a medium bowl. Stir until the mixture is **crumbly**.

4 Sprinkle mixture evenly over the pie filling. Cover the pie with aluminum foil. Bake for 15 minutes. Take the pie out of the oven. Turn the oven down to 375 degrees.

5 Remove the aluminum foil from the pie. Bake for 35 minutes or until the top is golden brown. Let the pie cool.

SWEET S'MORE BARS

Serve your family this twist on a favorite treat!

MAKES 16 BARS

INGREDIENTS

6 tablespoons butter

¼ cup brown sugar

6 tablespoons maple syrup

2 cups rolled oats

½ cup flour

¼ teaspoon salt

1 cup graham cracker crumbs

½ teaspoon cinnamon

1½ cups chocolate chips

1½ cups mini marshmallows

TOOLS

measuring cups

measuring spoons

8 × 8-inch baking pan

parchment paper

saucepan

mixing spoon

rubber spatula

microwave-safe bowl

pot holders

1 Preheat the oven to 350 degrees. Line the pan with the parchment paper.

2 Melt the butter in a saucepan over medium-low heat. Add the brown sugar and syrup. Stir and cook about 5 minutes or until the sugar **dissolves**. Take the saucepan off the heat.

3 Add the oats, flour, salt, graham cracker crumbs, cinnamon, and 1 cup chocolate chips to the saucepan. Stir well. Press the mixture into the baking pan.

4 Bake for 15 minutes. Take the pan out of the oven. Add the marshmallows in an even layer. Bake for 5 minutes. Let the bars cool.

5 Put the remaining chocolate chips in a microwave-safe bowl. Microwave for 30 seconds. Stir. Repeat until the chips are melted. Drizzle the chocolate over the bars. Chill the bars for 1 hour.

CONCLUSION

This book has some seriously **delicious dessert** recipes! But don't stop there. Get creative. Add your favorite ingredients to the recipes. Cook it your way.

Check out other types of home cooking. Make tasty soups, **salads**, main dishes, drinks, and even dips. Put together a meal everyone will cheer for.

WEBSITES

To learn more about Cool Home Cooking, visit booklinks.abdopublishing.com. These links are routinely monitored and updated to provide the most current information available.

GLOSSARY

batter – a thin mixture of flour, water, and other ingredients used in baking and frying.

crumbly – in small pieces.

delicious – very pleasing to taste or smell.

dessert – a sweet food, such as fruit, ice cream, or pastry, served after a meal.

dissolve – to become part of a liquid.

fluffy – soft and light.

permission – when a person in charge says it's okay to do something.

salad – a mixture of raw vegetables usually served with a dressing.

unique – different, unusual, or special.

utensil – a tool used to prepare or eat food.

INDEX